teddy bears 1 to 10

teddy bears 1 to 10

Written and Illustrated by
Susanna Gretz

Follett Publishing Company · Chicago · New York 🄵

Copyright © 1969 by Susanna Gretz. All rights reserved. No portion of this book may be reproduced in any form without written permission from the publisher. Manufactured in the United States of America. Published simultaneously in Canada by The Ryerson Press, Toronto.

First published 1969 by Ernest Benn Limited, London.

SBN 695-48460-5 Titan
SBN 695-88460-3 Trade

Library of Congress Catalog Card Number: 68-9563

First Printing

J

1 teddy bear

2 old teddy bears

3 dirty old
teddy bears

4 teddy bears
in the wash

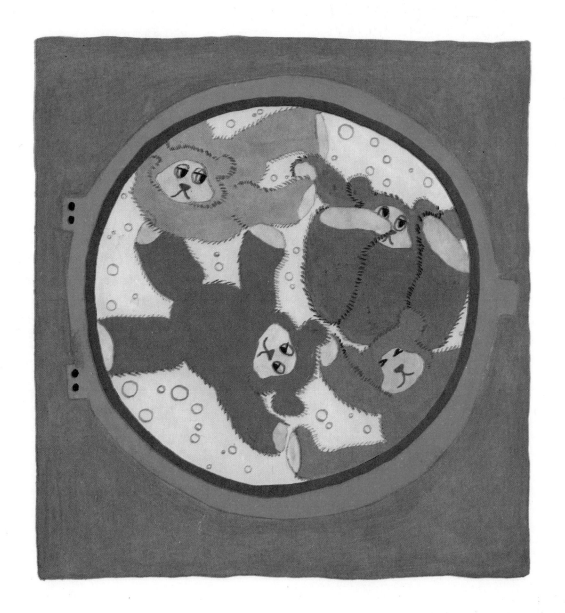

5 teddy bears
on the clothesline

6 teddy bears
on the radiator

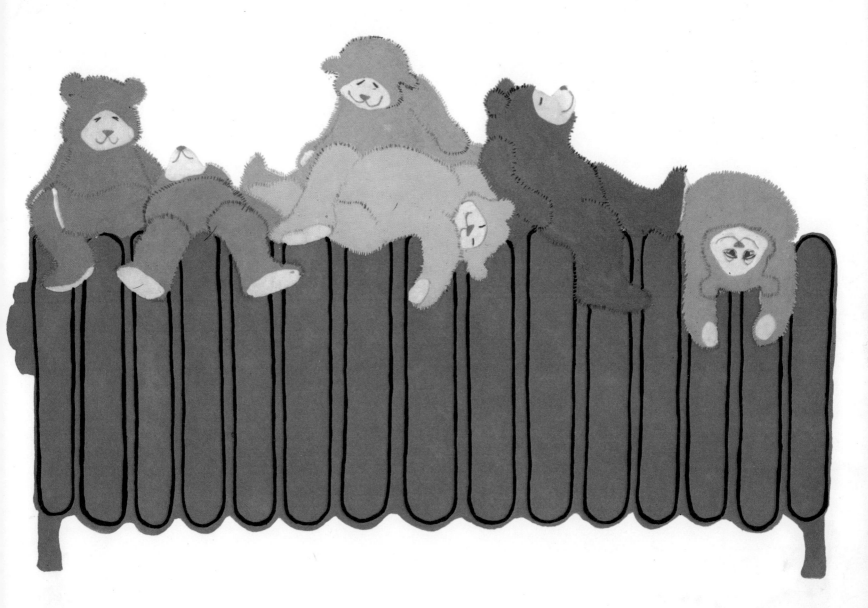

7 teddy bears
at the cleaner's

8 teddy bears
at the dyer's

9 teddy bears
on the bus

and 10 teddy bears
home for tea

Susanna Gretz

Susanna Gretz is a talented new author-illustrator, and *teddy bears 1 to 10* is her first picture book. She and her husband reside in London, England.